Brief Messages
to Father

To the most wonderful Dad! with much love, Pam

Brief Messages to Father

Edited by Bruce Taylor Hamilton

GIBBS·SMITH
PUBLISHER

SALT LAKE CITY

First Edition
02 01 00 99 98   5 4 3 2 1

This is a Peregrine Smith Book, published by
    Gibbs Smith, Publisher
    P.O. Box 667
    Layton UT 84041
    Orders: (1-800) 748-5439
    Visit our Web site at www.gibbs-smith.com

Cover design by Derek Lancaster
Book design by Leesha Gibby Jones

Printed and bound in the U.S.

LIBRARY OF CONGRESS CATALOGING-IN-PUBLICATION DATA

Hamilton, Bruce Taylor
Brief messages to father/edited by Bruce Taylor Hamilton—1st ed.
p.   cm.
"A Peregrine Smith book"—T.p. verso.
ISBN 0-87905-844-7
1. Fathers—Miscellanea. 2. Father and child—Miscellanea.
    I. Bruce Taylor Hamilton, ed.
HQ756.B735 1998
306.874'2—dc21   97-27646
                                   CIP

FOREWORD

How we remember our fathers, how we speak (or often not find the words) to them, how the gamut of emotions and remembrances about those figures who were the first men to influence our lives — all are embraced in this book of two hundred letters.

Spanning seven decades, the writers in this volume range from six to eighty years of age, and their short messages rainbow the spectrum of emotions that one human can feel about another. Yes, there is love, humor, thankfulness, and respect contained in these letters. However, there is also anger, pain, and the sense of abandonment. One writer wishes others the luck of having his father, another looks back over a long life at her "Dead Beat Dad." Coursing through all these reminiscences are referrals to hard work and adages and lives to be emulated.

The letters reproduced in this volume are the top two hundred winners chosen from thousands of entries in a letter-writing contest, the second annual English language "Brief Message from the Heart." Based on a successful series of contests started in the Japanese city of Maruoka-cho in Fukui Province, this volume offers you, the reader, the full spectrum of how we view our fathers.

The English language contest is cosponsored by The City of Portland, Oregon; Portland State University; The Maruoka-cho Cultural Foundation; and Infinity Group, a firm with offices in Portland and Japan.

BRUCE TAYLOR HAMILTON, AUTHOR AND CONTEST JUDGE
PORTLAND, OREGON

The two other judges are Professor Patricia Wetzel of Portland State University and Judith Van Dyke, a program coordinator at Portland State University.

$\mathcal{M}$y Bald Dad:
My dad is loving, loyal, true —
He's handsome, daring, debonaire.
And all of this, he does without
One solitary strand of hair.

—DOMINIC EBACHER, AGE 15

Dear Father,
You taught me to follow my dreams and
stand up for my beliefs. Why don't you
let me?

— PATRICK J. HIGBIE, AGE 17

She's gone.
Fifty years, seven kids.
I find you in your woods
behind the old house
Walking quickly
Eyes focussed ahead.
Chasing the past

— ROSALIE EDMONDS, AGE 40

*Once when we went to dinner,
I vowed that I would tell you,
"I love you." It was the
hardest thing I have ever done.*

— ART DeMURO, AGE 41

Nice guy, aren't you?
  I love you best in the world,
     so keep calm whatever may happen.
  I broke your prized video camera . . .
        last night . . .
                    —MISAKO NIIZATO, AGE 37

You terrified my friends, but never me. When you shouted, "If you're having fun, then stop it." I appreciated your joke.

— NORINE DRESSER, AGE 64

I'm not sure which is harder, to be a good father or a good son, but I do know teamwork made each easier.

— DUDLEY NELSON, AGE 53

$\mathcal{N}$ever been many words between us
but I massage your old feet like always
cold and stiff but gratefully given
and everything is all right
— CORRINE OLSON, AGE 48

Deliberately waking me at dawn for the rainbow trout, after midnight for stars in a desert sky, you taught me delights of the uncommon hour.

— DAVE CAMPBELL, AGE 59

Recently my father said, "I don't know if you will be around for my 90th birthday." I asked why? He responded, "Because you'll be 71."

— HARRY BLYTHE, AGE 68

*I remember
sitting in a bubbly bathtub,
you played songs for me
on your guitar. I remember
wishing everyone could
have you for a father.*

— MATTHEW FARGO, AGE 17

*You called me Aretê —
"Excellence," in Greek — and
with that loving gesture
gave me the precious gifts
of confidence, esteem, value
and a happy heart!*

— ARDYS V. ESERHUT, AGE 75

*I remember when I would bring home
friends who had no father at home.
Once I asked, "Please buy Jack shoes
for wrestling?" You did.*

— SHERI BLANK, AGE 40

Daddy
As I sit in your garden listening
to the ocean
I find comfort
I remember you best there
I think you are there

— KATHY SATY, AGE 43

Dear Father, I like it when you hug me, but when you kiss me, I feel like Jell-O. Do you?

— NATALIA DeMURO, AGE 7

My dad works very hard. He deserves much credit. Without my dad life would be difficult and plain.

— BRIAN BATES, AGE 14

*Dad, please don't clear your throat when
I talk with my boyfriend on the phone.
Please understand I love him
like my mom loves you.*
— ARIKA KATAHIRA, AGE 24

Dad, I know you're depressed. You have outlived all your closest friends. Remember . . . you must be the toughest son-of-a-bitch of 'em all!

— ART DeMURO, AGE 41

*Dad . . . You have a dislike for carrots,
don't you?
Between you and me,
    I'll give you my brussels sprouts
in exchange for your carrots.*

— MISAKO NIIZATO, AGE 37

*I suppose that if you didn't make those
funny noises when you eat,
then you wouldn't be my Dad*

— ROBIN BRIDGE, AGE 24

Because he is nice I love him
and he is sort of beautiful
I don't like his whiskers but I do love him
— SOPHIA GARDNER, AGE 6

Now that you are ninety-three
I've found your opportunity
To see Japan with Mom and me!
Let's make a splendid memory!
Pack the binoculars!
— JEANNIE EUNICE REYNOLDS, AGE 52

I understood the night you walked home twenty-five miles covered in sweat ashen-faced drooping shoulders weighted arms after your sawmill burned down

—Samuel Lee Smith, age 47

Dad,
When I tell my sons, "hold your horses,"
or "It's time to hit the hay!" I realize
something: I was listening after all.
— THOMAS RALPH NISSEN, AGE 42

*Dear Dad,
You are cool, neat, wonderful, and funny.
I love you a lot. Sometimes you yell at me.
I don't like that much. Alexis*
— ALEXIS BECKLEY, AGE 9

*No professor or textbook has prepared
me better than the man who slaved in the
sausage shop to show me the meaning of
"sacrifice."*
— DARRELL MARLATT, AGE 33

Little League, the Volkswagen Bug, fishing trips, shaving lessons, root beer floats outside, college advice, a graduation handshake—and that's just what everyone else has seen.

— HEATH A. KORVOLA, AGE 22

Although I never knew my father, you've made sure I never went wanting for fatherly love. I love you, Grandpa.

— BRANDON YOWELL, AGE 19

*How glad I am
you kept
your promise.*
— MICHAEL BACA, AGE 31

You, Borsalino at rakish tilt,
    stride jauntily into the hereafter.
I study your death mask,
honoring a noble profile,
musician's perfect pitch,
Father's educated heart.

—JUDITH BACHMAN, AGE 60

Dear Dead Beat Dad: Just wanted you to know what you missed—my first day of school, my first prom, my wedding day, your grandchild and now you're dead.

—D. L. STILL, AGE 80

New Year's when you gave me the keys to the car and said, "I trust you, have fun." I didn't have fun!

—CLAUDIA HUGHES, AGE 52

A trillion galaxies.
A billion stars.
Five billion people.
Two hundred countries.
Fifty states
Thirty-six counties.
Two parents.
One father.
One child.
Imagine it!

—STEPHEN BAUER, AGE 38

There when I needed you.
There when I wanted you.
There when I didn't want you.
Which was when I needed you
Most of all.

— STEPHEN BAUER, AGE 38

I miss you. Why didn't you cry when I
stepped on that plane to go halfway
around the world by myself? I love you.

— BLISS WOOLMINGTON, AGE 16

I don't know where you are, or even who.
But you gave me life.
And I know where I am, and who I am.
Thanks.

— STEPHEN BAUER, AGE 38

I love my dad because he works, he makes us money by setting tile, he sets the tile day and night and we love him.

— MARCUS STERLING, AGE 13

Just wanted you to know that you taught me the meaning of success is to follow your heart and chase your dreams!
— SCOTT BLACK, AGE 14

Dear Daddy,
We disagree, and I can't match your
1500 SAT score, but I know you
love me anyway. I love you too.

— LIZ HARPER, AGE 15

Just wanted you to know . . .
I've learned shame, hate, dispair, ridicule,
& destruction. I've learned love,
compassion, integrity, respect & care.
Have I learned enough to be your son?

— JAMES L. BRINDA, AGE 34

*The pictures of us on the mantel
that fell like old blooms
have risen again, father*

—JOSH AMRHEIN, AGE 22

It's hard when you're mad at me, but then I remember the good times we've had together and it puts a grin on my face.

— KEIRA SAGNER, AGE 7

Dear Dad,
Just wanted you to know . . .
Your recipe for wontons had held me all
winter long. Thanks.

— DAVID NOVAK, AGE 27

You always knew when it was better to
say nothing, to simply be there while I
worked things out for myself.
Thanks Dad!

— KARL CLARK, AGE 54

"Dad, can I go here?"
"Dad, can I go there?"
Then one day you said no,
But I went anyway—
And you wished me well.

— ART DeMURO, AGE 41

"Life is a grocery store. You can have
anything you wish. However, before you
leave, you must go by the cash register."
I'll remember, Dad.

— ART DeMURO, AGE 41

You are ordinary.
But something like the twilight sound
of crickets fills you,
echoing in your darker spaces—
even when you are no longer listening.
—HOLLY DeGROW, AGE 25

Dear Dad
You live happily, don't you?
I have continued to live.
Live and let live. So I am happy.
But I can't help thinking about you.
— CHIEKO NISHIZAWA, AGE 52

*For pets galore, for discipline
and laughter;
for playhouse, sandbox and swings,
handmade;
for the richest of childhoods,
this Depression-born daughter
thanks you Dad.*

— RUTH NISSEN, AGE 64

Dad, What you taught me, I am.
Sometimes it's hard.
You aimed so high —
love, Roberta

— ROBERTA GORG, AGE 56

Just wanted you to know . . .
the Japanese-English Dictionary you keep
in the bathroom taught me a lot.
Thank you.

— ANNA FIDLER, AGE 23

𝒯hanks to your invisible helps,
even I with handicap
could live a peaceful life with
a good wife and two nice kids.
— YOSHIO MAEDA, AGE 46

I wish I'd listened to you; being here behind bars is terrible. I'm sorry I've disgraced our family name.
I really miss you, Dad!

— KARL CLARK, AGE 54

Father,
We shared only brief times together.
Memories bitter, sweet, linger in my heart.
I feel you close by.
Goodbye, my Hero.
Lovingly, Carol
— CAROL ANN SAXTON, AGE 58

All my life, Dad asked,
"Who is the best?"
I am, I laughed.
Now you are gone—who was the best?
You were I cry.
— KATHLEEN HOLDEN, AGE 56

To prove that I was worthy of your love, I did no harm.

— H. G. LUCKY LIEBERMAN, AGE 62

Dad deserves this trip, by George! His heart is bigger than anyone you'll ever know. Adopted 10 children. Hardest working man. Reaches out to others.

— GERRY R. LOTT, AGE 43

I waited, an eager child,
but you didn't write
for too many years.
Now that you've died,
sorrow complicates my anger.
—SANDRA LEE BOUCHER, AGE 56

Dad: Everyone says how much I look like you. Well, we've taken different paths. In time, perhaps you'll also come to look like me.

—DAIGAKU RUMMÉ, AGE 45

"Thank you very much."
I have murmured many times toward
*   your back.*
"Go your way."
Your smile has always replied
*   to my heart.*

— NORIKO TAKAHASHI, AGE 37

Dear Dad,
　　Your excitement for life was contagious.
From you I learned love, loyalty and the
value of each moment lived.
　　　　Appreciative love, Elsie

—ELSIE RODMAN, OVER 65

*You taught me to lie. While courting
my mother you said you liked jazz.
I told my love I didn't eat meat.
It worked!*

— KEN UNKELES, AGE 44

*Daddy, do you know I sometimes
wrap your red plaid shirt around me
and pretend you're still with me—
You always show me the way—*

— DOTTIE DRYDEN, AGE 67

In college, when other kids received letters and money from their fathers, you would send me parables or philosophical tidbits; I saved them all.

— ART DeMURO, AGE 41

Plump
little
penguins
swathed in
blazing orange
peeking out
from your bookshelf
Pushkin
Blake
Voltaire
Thoreau
for this
magical
legacy
I thank you

— EILEEN BELLE, AGE 37

*Those who ride rainbows
and hear music from dusty trumpets,
know you are my dad.
Thanks for being you.*

— KARL CLARK, AGE 54

*We may not agree on everything,
but I love you anyway.*

— BETH SCHUSSMAN, AGE 13

—*Dad*
I love you so much. You go to work to get money so we won't starve and buy things for our fun
      —*Thanks*

—TARA ESPLIN, AGE 11

*Dad, Only once have I seen your tears,
the day when Grandmother passed away.
I remember that, forever.*

——JIEFAN LIAO, AGE 33

The sun still rises
But it's brighter when you're here
Please come back soon, Dad

—ERICA MEYER, AGE 13

I advanced to within two yards of
our enemy.
Captain, Gingerbread is on the table.
Give me next order . . . Dad?

—MISAKO NIIZATO, AGE 37

*In high school, you always brought home
my favorite corned beef & pastrami
sandwiches from the deli on Thursdays
after my late gym class.*

— Leonard Berman, AGE 30

*We mingled your ashes with Mom's
plus a huckleberry branch (for Mom);
we dropped them in your favorite
fishing spot*

— Dottie Dryden, AGE 68

Dear Dad,
Your sincere effort to explain to Yvonne
and I why our bodies were changing
endeared you to me for life.
You still stuttering?
> *Clevonne*

—CLEVONNE JACKSON, AGE 46

Dad—Even though you taught me not to—I cried the day you died. Sorry

— CRAIG THOMPSON, AGE 50

*Our time together, infrequent, miles
strung out, never taking us to the absolute
zero we knew that night on the road
between our birth towns*

— JOSH AMRHEIN, AGE 22

*You would never point in the direction
you intended; instead wisdom prevailed
as you guided me along with your fancy
footwork, you debonair Dad.*

— NANCY SHIRE, AGE 49

I had my watch engraved with the word, "Dad." Now, when I look at the time, it will always remind me of you.

Love,
Mark

— MARK JOHNSON, AGE 27

*Y*our imaginative, instructive conversations with inanimate objects using your unique dictionaryless vocabulary at random educated me on numerous topics while being entertained! What a gift!

— JEANNIE EUNICE REYNOLDS, AGE 52

Dad . . .
  I did it again!
    Mom is always nagging at me,
but I am sure
    it is Like father, Like ~~son~~ . . .
daughter!
— MISAKO NIIZATO, AGE 37

*My first step to take is to believe you.
But I cannot trust you without
objecting.
    I am at a loss what to do . . .*
                        — MISAKO NIIZATO, AGE 37

*Nothing you would ever do
    could be of the slightest interest to
    me.
I wish you had said just one word of
apology . . .*
— MISAKO NIIZATO, AGE 37

*That like a curled-up ladybug on freezing
nights . . . warm in her nest . . . happy
HAPPY . . . soaring upwards . . . like
under an umbrella . . . is you cuddling me.*
— MADELEINE KETTNER, AGE 12

Only faint memories still exist in my mind, perhaps created through the stories of my mother. I wish you were here with us.
Jim Seichi Watanabe 1935–1971

—STEVEN KAZOU WATANABE, AGE 26

Dad, you never hug me, you never say you love me, we both know we can't live together, but you will always be my father.

—MIYUKI WATANABE, AGE 30

I found an old letter from you yesterday. I laughed out loud at the words you wrote, and then I cried. I miss the laughter.

—SERENA BENSON, AGE 41

You're so wonderful, Dad, You should have a Baskin-Robbins ice cream flavor named after you.

—KARL CLARK, AGE 54

Thanks, Dad, for maintaining your composure and not screaming too loud as you taught your "baby girl" how to drive.
— HEATHER KENNEDY, AGE 31

I forgive you for not coming to my First Communion or college graduation — for being absent all my life, till your death.
— MARGARET CHULA, AGE 48

While the outside world is sleeping
You come knocking at my door
In your voice comes greeting,
"Wake up! It's half past four."
    You smile.

—LUIS JOSÉ RIVAS, AGE 15

As I look up to the sky, I remember you.
The beautiful sky I saw on my way to your
hospital is alive with you.

— HIROMI OGA, AGE 28

You were like the wind.
You were another place away from
my family.
So I couldn't touch and hold you finally.
I always missed you.

— HIROMI OGA, AGE 28

Please call me a daughter-in-law;
therefore, I can call you a father-in-law.
I really want to become your child.
— HIROMI OGA, AGE 28

$\mathcal{N}$o one but me knew it was you
in the dragon costume,
father, you always made me
laugh.

— JOSH AMRHEIN, AGE 22

Dad,
Do you like me? Do you miss me?
Do you think about me? Do you wish I
were never born?
> *Write soon*
> *Love, Kathryn*
> — KATHRYN GARDNER, AGE 34

Every time I get a room with a view,
you offer me a pair of binoculars.
Why the hell do you do that, Dad?
> — ROBIN BRIDGE, AGE 24

Dad—*Remember the arrowheads we found along the Columbia, rattlers' tails from The Dalles, agates from Wecoma? Still have 'em! Loved our treasure hunts.*
Alicia

—ALICIA TORREY, AGE 44

I cried too
as you held me
my last day home.
I cried again,
You said you miss me
and you love
who I've become.

— HEATHER BURNS, AGE 24

Dear Father
Thank you for your working hard.
Next time when we go fishing,
let's catch a whale.

— TSUJIKA SATO, AGE 17

Dear Father.
Please give me your smile
When I marry.

— YOSHIE KUDO, AGE 18

Dear father
Your big back is my country.

— TAKUMI HATAKEYAMA, AGE 18

*Dear Dad
Next Sunday
Let's have a date with me in secret.*
　　　　　　　　　—HARUMI NAKAMURA, AGE 17

$\mathcal{D}$ear Father,
I just wanted to tell you that even though
I only see you every other weekend
I think about you all the time.
—BRANDON WOODARDS, AGE 14

Father,
You make me feel knowledgeable even
when I'm ignorant because of how you
explain things to me. As an equal.
I love you.

—JENNIFER STICHMAN, AGE 14

Just wanted you to know your great-
grandchildren hear the gentle waterfall
created by the rock you placed in a small
creek three generations ago.
Love—

—CLAUDIA HUGHES, AGE 52

Hi Father,
The snow has been beautiful. Your garden took the surprise well, a good thing since I know nothing about vegetables. Thinning must wait for you.

—DANNY LEWIS, AGE 50

Dear Dad
Don't worry, I will try harder

—KATSUYUKI OBARA, AGE 16

*Dear Dad
Are you happy?
From Kaori*

—KAORI SAGAMI, AGE 17

Dear father
To say the truth. I dislike you because you
and mother are always arguing.
Please get along well with mother
That's my favor

— KUMIKO SASAKI, AGE 16

Thank you, Father. Every morning you drive me to the station. Buy the new car quickly.

— SEIKO SHIKA, AGE 15

People say, "You look like your mother," But I am my father's daughter.

— CHIYOMI SASAKI, AGE 16

Beloved Dad,
Inside, I cry, as I watch your courageous
struggle to get through each long day . . .
and longer night . . . without Mom.

— JULIE B. SIEGEL, AGE 65

Come to think of it,
You always put us first.
How stupid I was
To take your deep love as a
matter of course!

— MANAMI KOMADA, AGE 36

Together we were walking wordless. The furrows of your hand guided me to the cherry tree you'd planted for me. For everybody it flourishes.

—BRUGGER HANS PETER, AGE 42

Papa, I love wearing your oxford shirt—.
You wore it when mama died—.
I dug it out of the trash—.
I never told you—. Ciao. ♥

—CLAEBURN, AGE 45

Dad, you quarreled with my mother. But, I know you love her. When you come back from your business trip, give her some presents.

— KAORI OKA, AGE 15

I never forgot the time you fell, scraping your knee badly, trying to teach me to ride my bicycle. I love you, dad. Thank you.

— ANGELL R. JENNINGS, AGE 23

𝒟ear Daddy,
Thank you for the letters you wrote to me.
I've saved them all and read them aloud to
myself when I miss you most.

— CAROL ERDMAN

𝒯he relationship dad and I have is
important to me. He is a wildlife
biologist and teaches me to love the
animals of our world.

— TRAVIS W. LOWE, AGE 12

When my baby died, if you had not been there I wouldn't have lived through those days. You are the best. I love you.

—SUSAN HIGH, AGE 46

I'm doing just fine being me, not too many painful bruises, I'm getting a share of the pie, I'm eating well & warm at night.

—STANLEY KAMINSKY, AGE 46

When you left all those long years ago, you hurt me really bad, but your never comin 'round hurts me much more.

— LAURA BAKER, AGE 14

My dad is the best dad in the world because he always has time for me. No matter what, he loves me

— MIKEY SPENCER, AGE 9

That my dad isn't living with me. I love him because, I know he wouldn't hurt me. He is living with another woman.

— RYAN SHAWVER, AGE 9

My dad is rad. He's so bad. He's the best dad I ever had. But he left home and now I'm sad.

— KEVIN SHAWVER, AGE 12

*He makes me laugh, he makes me cry,
he makes me want to die.
I'm the only thing he's got
I love him . . .
Maybe not.*
　　　　　　—HANNAH M. THOMPSON, AGE 13

𝓜y dad is a dad who likes soccer and who works on houses and swims a lot. He makes treehouses and stuff and drives tractors.

— SHAD RENTSCH, AGE 9

𝓜y dad is Vietnamese. He escaped the war. A boat that came at night took him to freedom.

— LINNET MILLIKAN, AGE 10

*You may not be very tall outside,
but you are very big inside,
and I love you very much.*

— BRENT SMITH, AGE 12

I had a difficult time understanding you when I was young. Now that I have been to your homeland, I understand.

— NHIEN NGUYEN, AGE 21

All I ever wanted to do was make you proud of me. Now, I've realized you have worked so I can be proud of you.

— NHIEN NGUYEN, AGE 21

Just wanted you to know it's your turn to clean out the garage.

— LEAH KENAGY, AGE 21

𝒟ad, when I was 3, I knew all along . . . you could not fool me by pretending to be my Uncle Roy.

— YUKINA WARNER, AGE 33

*I see beauty and feel love to the corners
of my life because the farmer,
my father, showed me how to care for
even the edges.*

— JENNIFER SCHLOMING, AGE 45

*Warm belly-full of laughter
and cozy, flannel moments by the fire;
camping with you dad
was nourishment for a lifetime.*

— GREG STOLTZ, AGE 29

Dear Dad,
Recalling your absence during my
childhood makes me grateful for
your presence in my children's . . .
Welcome back!

— LARRY HURST, AGE 40

Every time I do the right thing
I give my Father the highest tribute
Giving back a small part of what he
has given me

— SUSAN TAMASHIRO, AGE 37

*Smart Detective, good husband,
salmon catcher, inventor, gem cutter,
storyteller, walking encyclopedia, athlete,
Checkers master, clam digger,
dragon-tatooed, tomato grower,
we love you.*

— REBA OWEN, AGE 55

*It was you who taught me to keep
still so time and wisdom could
grow within me.
You showed me that silence can
be strength.*

— DAVE CAMPBELL, AGE 59

Why didn't I see? Why didn't I say?
Sharing so much, am I not really you?
Now I see. Now I say. All too late.

—DEAN MEADORS, AGE 52

You are in my thoughts each day.
Every season brings new memories:
planting flowers, fishing,
rides to school, ice skating.
I miss you!

—LISA ROWAN, AGE 31

You're a very special man
I'm glad we've come this far
I'm proud of you and hope
I can be half the "mensch"
you are

— KARLA BENSON, AGE 41

Daddy, your granddaughters still cry at
the sound of a squeaky crutch — You've
been gone 17 years but you are in our
hearts always —

— DOTTIE DRYDEN, AGE 67

Dearest Dad—
I'm two . . .
you're loud, strong, tall, immortal.
I'm thirty-two . . .
you're quiet, weak, frail, dying.
I miss your laughter,
your wisdom, your love.
                    —KIMBERLY EL-JAMAL, AGE 35

I'm sorry we never said, "I love you,"
before you died thirty years ago, Dad.
Our generations never learned
to say it aloud; how sad.

— PAULINE WILLIAMS, AGE 65

While teaching, occasionally and accidently my young students call me "Dad." Invariably they are seeking advice, occupied with learning, and trusting. It is an honor.

— GERALD CARLSON, AGE 53

Dad, once I wondered why you left us; each autumn you went to sea. Now, as the west wind blows, I understand your lonely love.

— MARY J. MACKENZIE, AGE 63

*That I'm trying my best
to bring dignity to our
family, the way you did.
I think of you often.*

— LEAH STENSON, AGE 48

*Just wanted you to know, dad . . . despite
my graying hair, each tight embrace is
treasured. The gift? You are* always *the
last to let go. Jon*

—JON EDWARD KIPP, AGE 32

*$\mathcal{I}$ want to talk books, argue politics,
show you how well my kids turned out,
see you spoil great-grandchildren.
I miss you, Dad.*

—SUSAN M. BROWN, AGE 55

Whispering my aching hope
alone—a daughter.
These empty years
not knowing—
ageless, vibrant father—
your child, at sixty, weeps goodnight.
Searching newsreels. Loving.
—KAY SCHWARZ, AGE 60

That it was you who gave me the gift of wisdom, and now when you seek my advice, the words I speak come from you.

— BARBARA TAYLOR, AGE 43

After my attempted suicide, when the first thing you did was hold me tight against your chest, I was filled with undying love for you.

— ART WASHBURN, AGE 68

I'd have loved you, Dad!
You chose my wonderful Mother,
and she chose you.
I wish I had known you.

— HAZEL R. JUDD, AGE 82

My fury reaches a point of release.
My thanks, inadvertent teacher;
your intolerance and misdirected anger
my incentives to pursue acceptance
and patience.

— JERICHO KNIGHT, AGE 25

Fathers come,
Fathers go,
Some never show.

Of the three
The third happened to me.
How do I say —
Daddy, just wanted you to know?

—STEWART JONES, AGE 35

$\mathcal{M}$y sisters, 5½, 3½, wanted a brother when they heard attending physician say, "Mrs. Flood, this is your most beautiful daughter—looks just like you!" Dad became my best friend for life.

— NINA MARIE FLOOD VRTISKA, AGE 72

If I took all the magic of my childhood, a birthday candle, a shooting star, I'd wish you were alive again, just one more day.

— JOE V. ZAMUDIA, AGE 39

My shoulders are strong like yours. Silently they move. Up when angry. Down when happy. They speak the unspoken. Do you recognize the language?

— KATIE MILLER, AGE 27

Dear Dad, have I ever told ya how much I love you? I love you more than anything else loves anything else.
Love, Grant

— GRANT PERHAM, AGE 8

Disembarking from the plane bringing me home from Vietnam, into your arms, your tears fell, I cried for the first time in twelve months.

— PETER Z. CZUPRYK, AGE 48

"Are you comfortable?
Then we'll begin."
Your soft Irish accent wrapped me
in velvet,
the story began.
Your voice, your stories . . .
I'll remember always, Dad.
— GILLIAN NICOLETTI, AGE 16

All these years
I am your son
Sometimes it was
a bother
But I knew
I'd turn out right
because you are
my father

—STEVE KLEIER, AGE 41

On my wedding day, when you held my hand and said, "I will miss you."
I knew you meant I love you!

— PEGGY REED, AGE 43

If not for alcohol I could have loved you
a few times you abstained —
I loved you — the alcohol won —
I could have loved you —

—ROBERTA SHARP, AGE 61

*Shadow projected
on the walls walking with me
he, lit from within*

*lantern of support
encouraging his daughter
infinity wick*

—QIANA RICKABAUGH, AGE 24

*You taught me to take off my coat and make dust in the world;
at the same time you showed me how to watch clouds.*

—DAVE CAMPBELL, AGE 59

*You held my hand
    when I was young;
now that you're old
    I won't let go
        of yours.*

—LINDA ROBERTS-BACA, AGE 36

I wish I was around when you were my age, you know, nine.
I guess I just miss you is what I'm trying to say.

— BRIAN PITTMAN, AGE 32

You took time to talk with me. You respected my opinions. You taught me that each person is individual. You live on in my life.

— ROMAINE L. RESNICK, AGE 77

Though you are gone, I remember you in the essence of jasmine, the beauty of a flower, the majesty of a tree, and your love.

— GWEN LAWRENCE, AGE 57

If I could have a thousand Dads
in any age that's past
None of them could make me
half as glad
as you have, Dad ♥

— MICHAEL JOHN BACA, AGE 31

Daddy,
I do not know how to speak the words
"I Love You" in Cambodian but I pray
that you hear them in my actions.
— ROBERT OLAN, AGE 19

You've taught me so many lessons, given
me so much . . . if only you'd taught me
how to love you without feeling like such
a clutz.
— MAUREEN LEE, AGE 44

I've spent my life proving that I am
as strong and independent as you,
but all I wish now is to be close to you.
— NHIEN NGUYEN, AGE 21

They all called you crazy.
I only know
you always fought for justice
for all.
If that's crazy,
I want to be crazy too.
— ELAINE LINDBERG, AGE 50

Because of you
  I'm unmarried.
Because of you
  I'm alone.
I can't find a man like my father.
Are you sure you don't have a clone?
          —LORI J. THOMAS, AGE 35

Time went on without you
years passed
I am now 23
if I look closely
I can still see your smile
you seem so tall

—HILARY CAMPBELL, AGE 23

*Dad, I keep looking for the end of the
rainbow, thinking you might be there
Where are you? I am here
Waiting —*
— E. SUZANNE MARTINEK, AGE 45

*Haiku
From your broad shoulders
I learned to see as far
as I could dare to dream*
— DAN BALMER, AGE 38

Dearest Dad
Haikei Please dream of me
as I will dream of you
*   from U.S.A.   Keigu*
*   Affectionately,*
*   Takashi*
                    —TAKASHI YAMADA, AGE 22

Your silence brought me solace,
taught me to listen is to learn.
But, after twelve years without you,
the silence is a painful roar.

— TERESA SEIBERT, AGE 33

Just wanted you to know—I forgive you for giving me away.
But then you said, "I Love You."
That's all I ever needed.

— CONNIE SMITH, AGE 63

It's my turn to show you our world. Drop by your post office, pick up a passport application. Prepare now. Join us abroad in 1997.

— MARIPAT HENSEL, AGE 38

As a child and bad,
I was told I was like you.
At twenty I met you and found, I'm proud
to be like you.

—SALLY BROWN, AGE 58

You taught me about ladybugs
when I was a little girl.
Then you died.
Now, when I see a ladybug,
I know you are near.

—ALLISON HUTCHINSON, AGE 46

You could give me life, but not your heart.
We shared a house and a name, but
nothing more.
And now . . .

Who were you, Father?
—SHEILA M. MAGEE, AGE 47

You live on in my life.
*   You provided the standard*
*   I live by.*
The sense of fairness, I judge with
*   And love to insulate me*
—NANCY THORNTON, AGE 59

Some called you eccentric—
But I knew that you were just yourself.
And you were honest and special and fun.
And you were my Dad.

— CAROL A. SAMPSON, AGE 45

You collected used clothes
And (inexplicably) Peugeots
You loved anything that was cheap.
And, although hardly inexpensive,
You also loved me.
Thanks, Dad.

— CAROL A. SAMPSON, AGE 45

Dad, I still remember you letting your little girl warm her hands inside your shirt as we pedalled homeward in Nagoya's sudden, swirling snow.

— TESS BOHNAKER, AGE 13

Whenever I begin taking you for granted, Dad, I simply turn and observe a silent, empty chair, and remember what life would be without you.

—Will Bohnaker, Age 54

A father who stands for achievement . . . can always expect a son trying for one better!

—Brett Seelig, Age 29

"Rhythms"

She remembered push-ups and prowess.
A military man.
Now, after a heart attack,
a slower walk,
no more pushing.
Finally, time for love.

—SHEILA STEPHENS, AGE 48

Oh, My Pa-Pa,
to me he was so wonderful,
deep in my heart
I miss him so today.
—CHE-CHEN C. GWO, AGE 43

I love how you're my baby girl's grandpa; especially that it was once me in her place and that someday I'll be in yours. Thanks

—SUSAN SCHIMELFINING, AGE 33

You loved me enough
To allow me to learn
Through my choices
Even when I broke your heart
You only seemed to love me more.
— KELLY MORRISON, AGE 34

Daddy
Stumbling down the stairs,
tears staining my face,
you hug me
fix my chair
brew me tea
and read.
Comforting me,
creating an irreplaceable bond.

— MICHELLE SCHROEDER, AGE 23

When you were young, dark-haired and hurried, you were my hero.
Now, silver and slower, you are my best friend.

— CINDY MILLS, AGE 49

You called me "Stormy." I am.
After all, I'm your daughter.
But there's always a rainbow after
the storm!
I loved you, Dad.

— CLAUDIA HUGHES, AGE 52